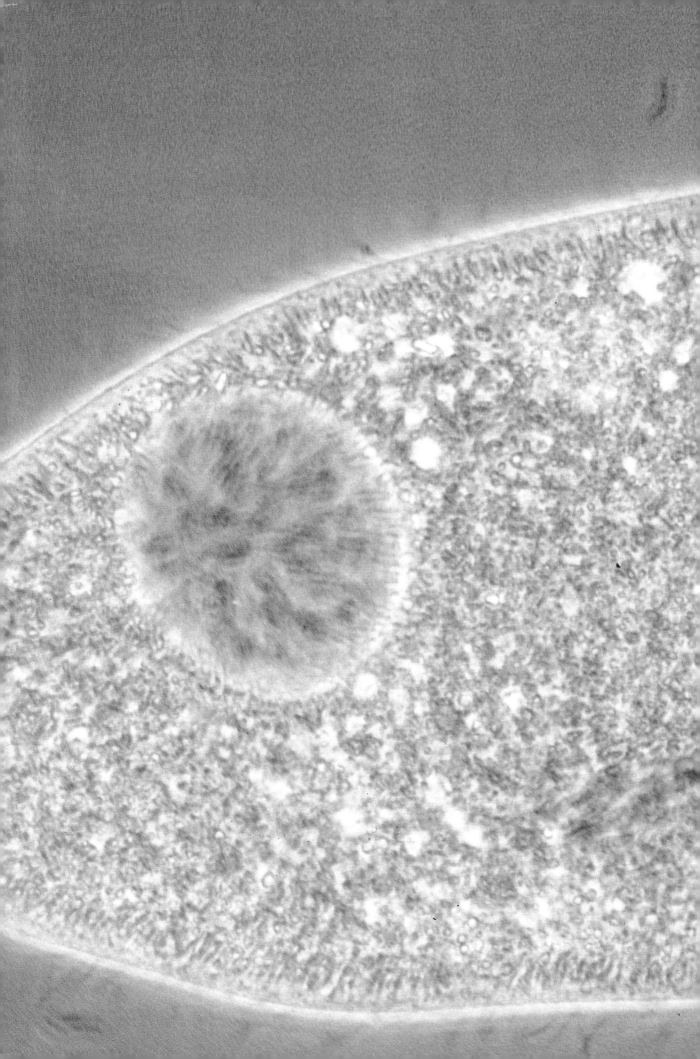

The
ZOO
in you
Discover the animals which live in you

David Taylor & Mike Birkhead
& Alastair MacEwen

Introduction

The warmth, moisture and freely available food that our bodies afford are very attractive to certain creatures. Some have become highly adapted to living in us and indeed can't do without us; I suppose if they could write they would describe us as their Earth, a planet where there is a great variety of different types of scenery and places to live, but all in all fairly welcoming. Though some of these animals are good lodgers who cause no offence, keep things tidy and even, in a way, pay their rent, others are undesirable guests with very bad manners.

At any given moment, the beasts that spend their days riding around in and on you number many millions. Imagine you're just going to pay a visit to this personal zoo and that this is your guide-book to a few of the amazing species on show – but I should warn you that before we set off we'd better shrink in size, because most of the zoo animals here are rather on the tiny side!

First published in Great Britain in 1987
Reprinted in paperback 1989
by Boxtree Limited

Text copyright © 1987 by David Taylor
Photographs copyright © 1987 by Mike Birkhead and
Alastair MacEwen

British Library Cataloguing in Publication Data

Taylor, David, *1934–*
Zoo in you
1. Man. Parasites
I. Title
616.9′6

ISBN 1-85283-255-X

Edited by Graham Eyre
Designed by Grahame Dudley
Typeset by Servis Filmsetting Limited, Manchester
Printed and bound in Italy by OFSA S.p.A.

for Boxtree Limited, 36 Tavistock Street,
London WC2E 7PB

Acknowledgements
Photograph on p. 8 courtesy of Bruce Coleman Ltd.,
on p. 10, 21 London School of Hygiene and Tropical
Medicine (Electron Microscopy Laboratory), p. 25
Mansell Collection, p. 43 London School of Hygiene
and Tropical Medicine (Dept. of Medical
Protozoology).

Contents

Abbreviations

mm   millimetre
cm   centimetre
m   metre
km   kilometre
ha   hectare
gm   gram
kg   kilogram

Bacteria

The world is literally teeming with germs, which we call microbes. One form of microbe is the *bacterium*, which many scientists consider to be a lowly form of plant. Bacteria are living creatures composed of a single cell. A human being is made up of many millions of cells, so it is not surprising that you cannot see a bacterium without the aid of a powerful yogurt, for grape-juice to turn into wine, and so on. They break down and build up millions of different substances. They create nitrogen in the soil, making it fertile so that it grows the plants on which you and all living creatures depend. You carry thousands of millions of them on and within your body. To them you are their world. To you they are part of your personal zoo, and most

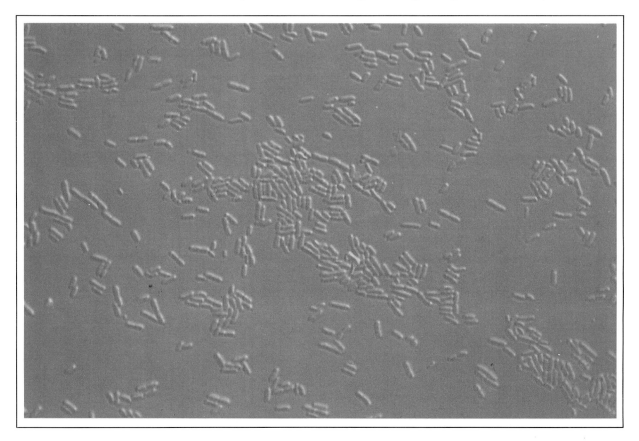

Bacteria under the microscope

microscope. Bacteria are measured in microns (1 micron is 1 millionth of a metre), and they can be found everywhere, from the bottom of the ocean to the top of mountains, in the air, in the soil, and inside plants and animals.

Many bacteria are harmless, friendly and very useful. Life on earth would be impossible without them. They are tiny chemical wizards, organizing all sorts of chemical reactions. They help you digest your food so that your body can use it. They help make it possible for milk to become butter, cheese and

of the time, I hope, you should get on well together. But sometimes things go wrong or unfriendly bacteria enter the body, and this is when you fall ill.

Bacteria may be plants, but they aren't green as they contain no chlorophyll, which is what plants need to obtain food from the air. It may be that bacteria are closely related to those other non-green plants the *fungi*. They come in a variety of shapes but there are three main designs: round ones called *cocci*, rod-shaped ones called

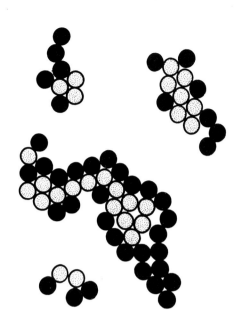

Coccus bacteria

bacilli and spirally twisted ones called *spirilla*. As I have said, some cause illnesses. *Staphylococci* are cocci that cause 'boils' in human skin. One form of bacillus causes tuberculosis, a disease of the lungs, and one type of spirillum

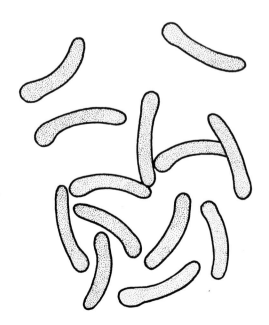

Bacillus bacteria

causes a kidney disease of dogs.

Bacteria multiply by dividing into two without any need for mating, as there are no males and females. The rate at which bacteria multiply is very fast and becomes faster the warmer it gets. If it takes 30 minutes for a bacterium of a certain species to divide into two, and that rate is kept up, one such bacterium will multiply into 1000 million bacteria within 15 hours! (But remember how small they are: a single teaspoon could hold 160,000 million bacteria of average

Spirillum bacteria

size.) Why, then, don't bacteria swamp the world? First, there isn't enough food around for them to keep multiplying at the same rate all the time. Secondly, as they increase in numbers their waste-products (particularly acids) increase, and this slows down the speed at which they can multiply.

In order to live, bacteria need moisture, warmth and food. Their surroundings must contain at least 4 per cent water, while the minimum

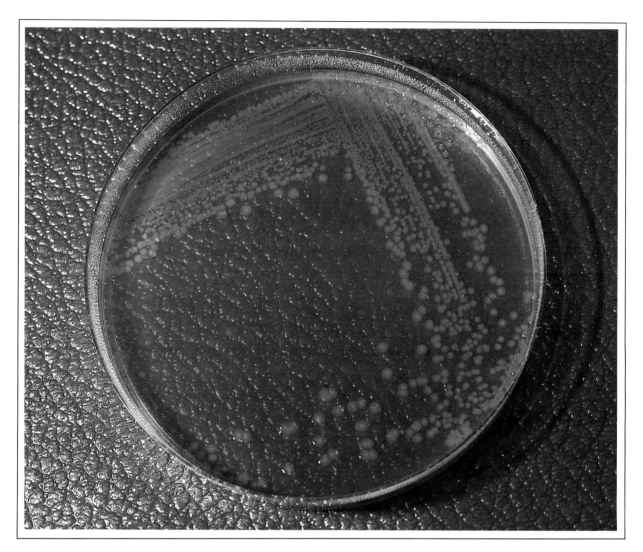

Bacteria growing on a jelly plate

temperature they require depends on the species. Some bacteria can obtain chemicals from the air and most need a source of nitrogen, together with tiny quantities of other chemical elements that are readily available throughout nature. Although some bacteria need oxygen, others can survive *without* it. Most bacteria prefer darkness to light, and direct sunlight kills most species.

At least 80 different kinds of bacteria live harmlessly in your mouth, and the total that leave your body every day when you go to the toilet ranges from an amazing 100 thousand millions to an even more staggering 100 million millions! The bacteria that make you their home are to be found on nearly every surface of the body that is open to the air or that can be reached from the outside through passages in your body. Many of these bacteria are not parasites, which have to live on you to be able to survive, but are simply lodgers taking advantage of the darkness, warmth, moisture and plentiful food that they find there. Other bacteria living on man are true parasites, unable to live anywhere else in nature. They have a special relationship with the surfaces of our bodies and, when things go wrong, can go through the surfaces into other parts of the body, where they are attacked and destroyed by the amazing array of defence systems built into the body. If they can overcome these defences for a while, they cause illness. Don't forget *all* healthy animals and plants have bacteria growing on their surfaces.

The body's defences against invasion by germs are many and varied. The strong acid of the stomach juices and the tears of the eyes contain chemicals that kill germs. Coughing helps to protect the breathing system from bacteria in the air, and so do the small hairs in the nose and the fine hairs on the bronchial (breathing) tubes of the lungs. Any unwanted bacteria that get inside the body are detected at once by the body tissues (the layers of cells that make up the various parts of your body), which send special sentry cells to the spot to fight and gobble up the germs. The body also uses special chemicals called 'antibodies' that are found in the blood and other body fluids. These have the power to lock onto and destroy invaders.

Large numbers of bacteria occur naturally on your skin. There are more in some places than in others. The hairless parts of the face and hands do not have very many, but sweaty and oily places such as the corners of the nose and the spaces between the toes have a lot. The navel or 'belly button' isn't overcrowded, but there are plenty of bacteria in the opening to the ear. The biggest numbers are found in the groin (where your legs join) and the armpits.

The bladder and the urethra (the place where urine is stored and the tube through which is passes out of your body) are usually sterile, which means free of bacteria. Urine becomes contaminated with bacteria only after leaving the body, as do sweat and saliva once they have left the glands that produce them. Saliva picks up bacteria in the mouth, and in a healthy person one spit contains 100–1000 million bacteria per cubic centimetre. Most clean skin contains around 5 million bacteria per square centimetre, which makes a total of 100,000 million germs on the skin of one adult!

Only when the resistance of the body to disease breaks down can some of the germs that normally live on your skin and any others that happen to land on you manage to break through the defences. These defences can be weakened if you are too cold, if you are not eating the right food and don't have all the vitamins you need, if you are already ill or have cut yourself badly. If you need extra help to fight off bacteria, the doctor may decide to use antibiotics, chemicals mostly developed from germ-killers found naturally in certain species of fungi.

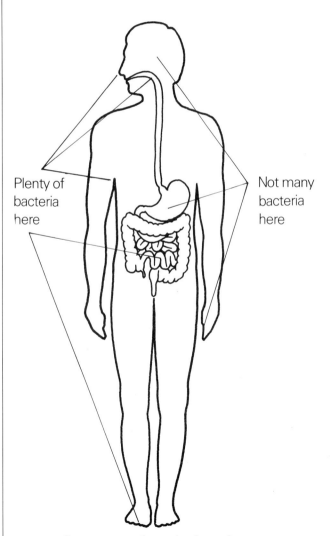

Plenty of bacteria here

Not many bacteria here

Some parts of your body are home to more bacteria than others

The Virus

In the zoo in you, the smallest inhabitants, far tinier than bacteria, are a strange and important group of creatures called viruses. These are so small that they are measured in nanometres (1 nanometre is 1 thousand millionth of a metre or 1 thousandth of a micron). The trouble is, we are not absolutely sure whether

Viruses come in a variety of shapes: some are round, some are shaped like loaves, some have rod-like bodies, and some are hexagonal (with six sides). In some ways they behave like non-living objects: for example, they can be turned into crystals, in the same way as non-living things such as sugar or salt can. In other ways they are like living

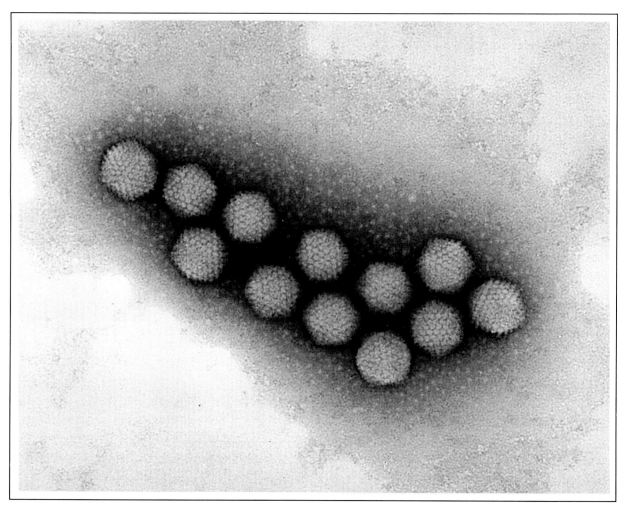

Adeno-viruses magnified 120,000 times

these things are dead or alive! (You'll see what I mean in a moment.)

Viruses can only grow in an animal or plant cell and have bodies composed of a core of acid covered by a coat of protein and sometimes some fatty and starchy material. They are so very tiny that you cannot see them with your student microscope, and no other microscope that uses light is any use either. They can only be seen with an electron microscope.

organisms: for example, they can multiply themselves. To do this they first attach themselves to, and then enter, a living animal or plant cell. Once inside they multiply by using the chemicals already in the cell to make more viruses like themselves. This means that viruses can only be grown in laboratories if they are provided with living cells that they can enter. These cells can be either those of living animals or plants, or those of what are called 'tissue cultures'. Tissue cultures are colonies of living cells that are kept alive in special 'soups' of nourishing liquids.

Sometimes viruses can live inside a cell without causing any trouble. They appear to be inactive or 'dormant'. 'Cold-sore' viruses may remain dormant for months or years in this way within the cells of your lips. They are 'woken up, it begins to multiply and damages or kills the cell. In the case of the cold-sore virus, the cell-damage results in tingly little blisters in the skin.

The body has a number of good defences against virus attack. These include the production of antibodies, which, as we saw when looking at bacteria, are chemicals that circulate in the blood and other body fluids and attach themselves to invaders and destroy them. They can do this also with

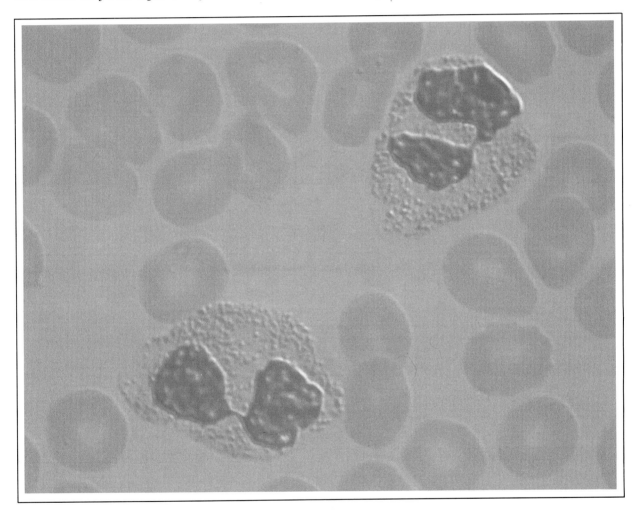

up' when the cell's resistance to attack is weakened. This may happen when you catch a cold or suffer from other illness, or when the cell is affected by something such as bright sunlight. (Cold sores tend to flare up when people who carry the virus go on holiday to a hot country or spend a lot of time in the sun.) When the virus has been woken

Blood magnified. The two white cells in the picture attack bacteria but are no defence against viruses

viruses. Also, cells infected with viruses make a special substance called 'interferon', which can spread to healthy cells and protect them by 'interfering' with a virus's ability to enter a cell and multiply. Viruses cannot be attacked by antibiotics, which are used to fight bacteria, but are often used when people or animals have virus diseases so that bacteria can't take the chance to make things worse. In this way, the body is protected from further infections and can concentrate on getting rid of the viruses.

Like bacteria, viruses can be turned into vaccines, which are usually fed into the body by injections and help protect humans and animals against disease. A vaccine for viral infections is made either by using a dead virus or, more often, by using one that has been weakened in the laboratory so that it cannot cause disease even though it is still alive. When given to the patient, the vaccine does not produce illness but *does* stimulate the body to produce defensive antibodies. These antibodies circulate in the body for a long time after vaccination and, even when their level in the blood falls, the body cells remember how to make them should viruses that haven't been weakened ever attack the body.

Your pet animals also can fall ill from diseases caused by viruses. There are viruses that are specially likely to attack them. Dogs can be attacked by viruses that cause liver disease or distemper, for example. Cats can suffer from viruses that attack the liver, cause diarrhoea or produce cat influenza (the sort of 'flu' that affects cats). It is wise to have puppies and kittens vaccinated against these viruses just as human babies are vaccinated against the virus that causes poliomyelitis or 'polio' – a killer disease that thanks to vaccination is now very rare. As a vet, I often see and treat viral diseases in all sorts of animals, ranging from dolphins to gorillas and elephants to falcons. Sealions are particularly at risk from a virus that causes a skin disease rather like chicken-pox, which is also caused by a virus. I have seen orang-outang

babies with measles caused by the same virus as infects children with this disease.

Reptiles, amphibians, fish, insects and even bacteria can all be infected by certain kinds of virus. Plants have a wide range of their own viruses, many of which cause them to become deformed. There are for example viral diseases of the tobacco plant and the potato. One of the worst viral diseases that can attack man is rabies. This horrible disease is usually caused by being bitten by a mad dog, but, thanks to very strict laws about taking

Some viruses and things they can cause

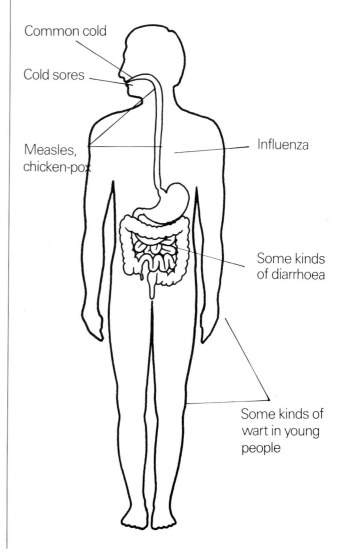

Orang-outangs can catch measles

animals from one country to another, it hardly ever occurs in Britain. Other bad viral diseases include the tropical disease yellow fever, and smallpox, which used to be common in Europe and America but has now just about died out because of the use of vaccines. If you are travelling to a country where some of the worst viral diseases are still found, you will have to be vaccinated against them before you go.

Where did viruses come from? Some scientists have suggested that they arrived here on earth from outer space in showers of dust from comet-tails and small meteors. A much more common idea is that they developed from the cores of plant or animal cells themselves. A third possibility is that they are remnants of more complicated parasites that got into the habit of living inside cells and eventually lost more and more bits of their original bodies as they came to rely more and more on the host cell.

The Fungus

Some fungi are able to make their home on or in the human (or animal) body. Fungi are a large group of plants which include some of the most primitive forms of plant life known to science. Unlike most plants, they contain no chlorophyll, the green chemical that helps plants to make food

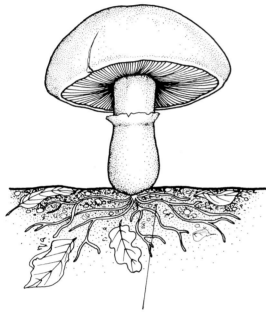

The fungus lives off dead or dying matter

A fungus's body plan

from the gas in the air called carbon dioxide. This process, known as 'photosynthesis', can occur only in daylight. Fungi cannot make their food in this way, so they have to obtain it from dead or decaying animal or plant material or, far less commonly, from living animals or plants. The type that live on dead or decaying cells are called 'saprophytes' while those that depend on living things are 'parasites'.

Fungi are a large family containing hundreds of thousands of species and are very widespread. However, they don't like direct light, or places that are too hot, too cold, too wet or too dry. They grow best in places that are dark, damp and fairly warm.

Fungi are constructed either as microscopic single cells or as branching tubes or filaments known as 'hyphae'. Some of the simplest fungi reproduce from cells called 'spores', which are sometimes clustered together within rounded containers called 'spore-sacs' or 'spore bodies'. The spores split off and start a new plant. More advanced fungi also produce spores, but only do so after male and female cells have joined together.

Although the individual fungus cell is invisible to the naked eye, it can be observed easily using a simple microscope. When large numbers of the cells are present in one place, the crowd can be seen without a microscope, as a white or coloured 'mould'. You have probably seen the moulds that grow on

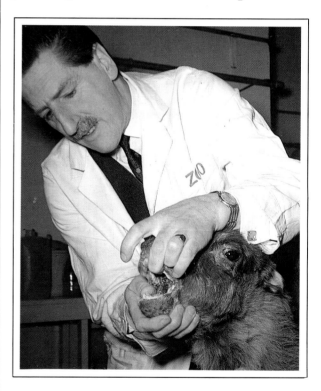

'Thrush' fungus in a baby camel's mouth

stale bread or old jam, and are sure to know the edible mushroom, which is another type of fungus. None of these fungi live in or on human beings. Only a very few species have the knack of surviving among the cells of our bodies,

and most of these only do so rarely, even though the spores of fungi are everywhere, blowing about in the air and continually landing on us without our ever seeing them.

Some of the fungi that can live in our bodies usually live in nature as saprophytes, preferring dead or decaying matter. One such is a kind of yeast-type fungus called *Candida* (Latin for 'white'), which causes the condition known as 'thrush' – white spots that often appear in the mouths of babies, particularly when they are being bottle-fed. I've even seen it in baby camels! The spots are actually masses of tiny, branching fungal hyphae. Candida is found naturally in the skin and mouth of human beings, and also in the lining of the alimentary tract (the tube that starts at the mouth and continues with the gullet, stomach and bowels to the opening called the anus, through which the body's waste passes). It can only cause trouble when the body's natural

A toadstool is a fungus

Saprophytes live on dead stuff

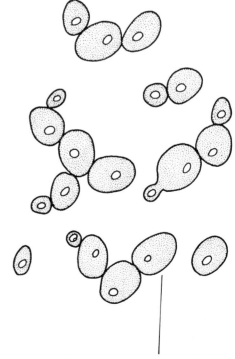

Under a microscope saprophytes look like this

defences are weakened for some reason.

Some fungi live in the human skin if they get the chance. One example is 'ringworm', which has nothing to do with worms but is caused by fungal hyphae that attack the outer layers of skin cells, hair and nails. Some of these fungi are picked up after contact with infected cats, dogs or cattle. Another fairly common fungus ailment is 'athlete's foot'. This again is caused by a species which lives on the skin of the feet, particularly between the toes, and which under normal conditions causes no trouble whatsoever. It only breaks into the skin when conditions are right for it: for example, when the skin is very sweaty or when you don't dry your feet properly with a towel. It is often found in the damp conditions of changing-rooms and swimming-baths and can live for a long time in socks and shoes.

More serious but rare diseases caused by fungi occur in other countries. In South Africa, pot-holers sometimes develop a fungal infection of the lungs after visiting caves where there are large numbers of bats. The fungus lives as a saprophyte on the bats' droppings and the men breathe it in through the air. Another kind of rare fungal disease occurs sometimes in Madagascar, off the coast of Africa. This is a fungus that

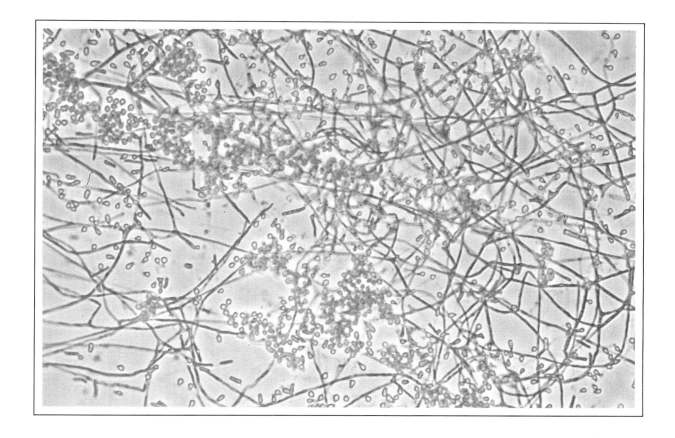

Ringworm fungus in human scalp

usually lives as a saprophyte on wooden posts but that under certain conditions can enter a human body and cause lung disease.

The temperature of the human body stops most fungi from establishing a home there. 37°C, the normal temperature of the human body, is too hot for them. Many actually die at a temperature of 40°C. Some fungi, such as the one that can cause ringworm, manage to avoid the high temperature of the inside of the body by only living

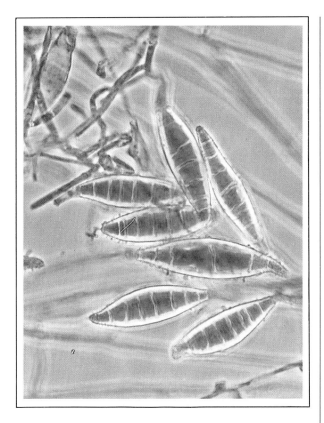

The pretty spores of a fungus causing ringworm in dogs

the body and they run riot and cause infections. Luckily new medicines that specifically attack fungi have been discovered and are now used by doctors to treat fungal infections when they occur.

One of the most serious fungal illnesses that affects animals is a type of pneumonia (a lung disease) suffered by birds. Young turkeys, penguins and falcons are particularly at risk from it. 'Thrush' may sometimes attack dolphins. Fungi also cause a number of plant diseases, such as potato blight and mildew.

The human body

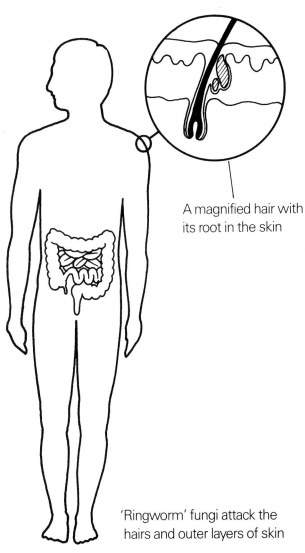

A magnified hair with its root in the skin

'Ringworm' fungi attack the hairs and outer layers of skin

on the outer layers of the skin and hair, which are cooler. The oil naturally produced by glands in the skin (the sebaceous glands) protects the skin from fungal (and some bacterial) infections. The natural fat is broken down by friendly bacteria living on the skin into fatty acids that make it difficult for fungi to grow. Friendly bacteria help the body to keep down fungal growth in other ways. The bacteria that live in the intestines help to keep in check the fungi that live there by competing with them for living-space and food, and sometimes they actually feed upon them. As on the skin, the bacteria may also produce chemicals such as acids that the fungi do not like.

Antibiotics, the medicines that have proved to be so good at fighting bacteria, do not kill fungi. This means that sometimes, if you take antibiotics for a long time, there are not enough bacteria left to keep down the fungi in

The Amoeba

You will need a microscope to introduce yourselves to the thousands of little lake-dwellers that live happily inside your intestines, paddling about in the dark where there is all the moisture, warmth and food that they could possibly want. These throughout the world, while others live only in certain surroundings. Some form part of the plankton (a sort of 'soup' of tiny living things that fish and other creatures feed on) in the oceans. Over 30,000 living species are known to science. They come in an amazing

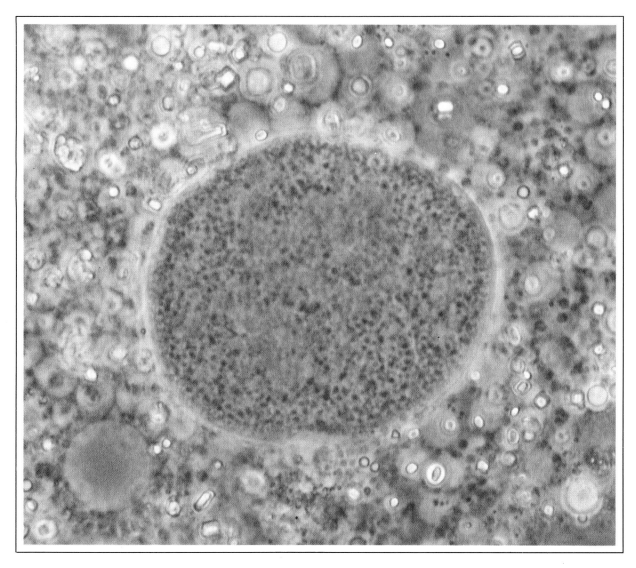

Amoebae highly magnified

harmless little individuals that spend their lives in the long winding tube from the stomach to the bowels are *protozoa*.

Protozoa are mostly microscopic one-celled creatures that should be classified perhaps half-way between animals and plants. They are found everywhere where there is moisture, in numbers almost as great as those of bacteria. Some species are found

variety of body shapes – from tiny blobs 2 microns long that live within the red blood-cells of animals to the delicate *foraminiferans*, with shells 5 cm across.

Some move by flowing and oozing, others paddle with rows of little 'oars' (cilia) and other wriggle and push themselves along with the aid of a 'tail' (flagellum). Some contain the green

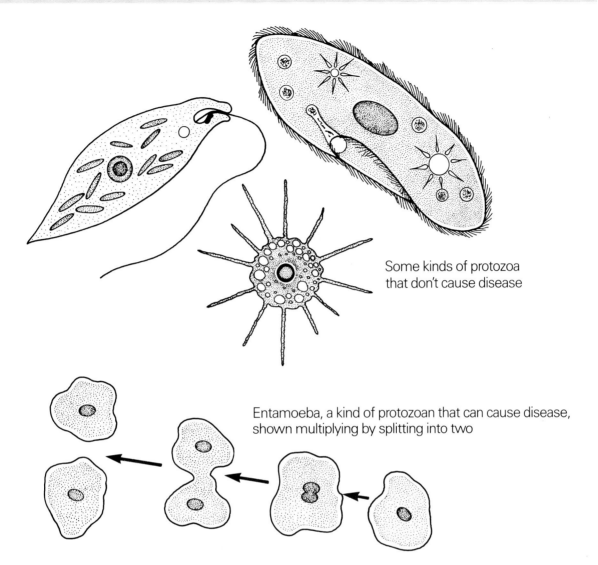

Some kinds of protozoa that don't cause disease

Entamoeba, a kind of protozoan that can cause disease, shown multiplying by splitting into two

chemical chlorophyll and in daylight can build up starchy foods from simple chemicals around them, and are important links in the food-chain of the ocean. Others live in the soil and feed on bacteria. And, while nearly all the protozoa are 'free-living' (not dependent on other living creatures as parasites) a very few cause disease by living as parasites.

Every biology student is familiar with the free-living *Amoeba proteus*. This tiny protozoan barely visible with the naked eye is found in pond-water. It has no fixed shape, but constantly changes its outline by pushing out parts of its single-cell body. The rest of the body then flows into the spaces left by the parts pushed out and in this way the amoeba moves along. The name given to

The variety of protozoans

the parts pushed out is 'pseudopodia' – Greek for 'false feet', which describes their use very well. The amoeba also uses its pseudopodia to flow round and trap food material in tiny holes which digest the food.

Like bacteria, amoebae multiply by splitting into two. Each of the two parts takes half of the 'nucleus' or core of the old cell. Large numbers of amoebae can be quickly produced by this splitting-process.

Various kinds of amoebae live in the human intestines quite naturally. They live and feed in a very similar way to the *Amoeba proteus* in its pond. Most measure only about 20 microns across. One species that is often present is

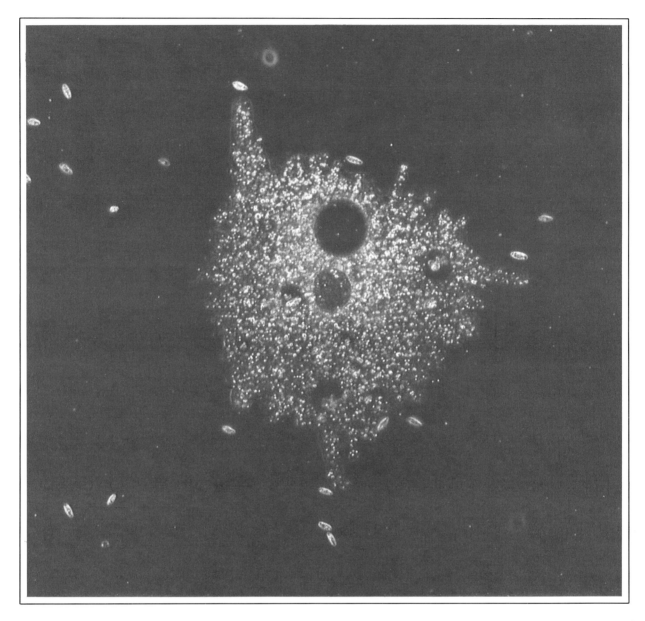

A pond amoeba

Entamoeba histolytica. Like other amoebae that live in the intestines, it usually feeds harmlessly on bacteria and other foodstuffs that are always present there, but sometimes, for reasons we do not understand, it becomes a dangerous parasite and begins invading the bowel wall, feeding on the tissues and red blood-cells and causing fever, pain and diarrhoea. This sudden bad behaviour by *Entamoeba histolytica* is more likely to occur in tropical and sub-tropical regions of the world, especially in unhygienic conditions. The disease that is caused in this way is called amoebic dysentery.

When *Entamoeba histolytica* leaves the body, it turns into a small, round object called a cyst. Such cysts do not move around by means of pseudopodia but contain 4 nuclei instead of 1 and are enclosed in a protective jacket. The *Entamoeba* cysts lie safely doing nothing in water or on the ground until taken in by another person through infected food or water. They can be carried onto food by flies. Once the cysts are inside a human being, their jackets dissolve, the 4 nuclei divide to make 8 and then the rest of the cell

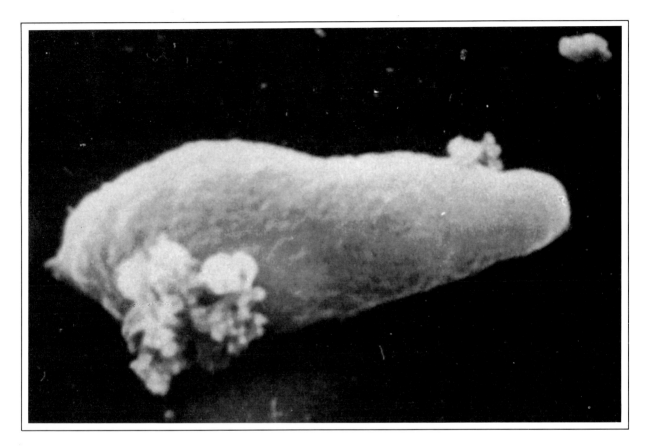

divides, producing 8 small amoebae which make their home in the intestine.

Amoebic dysentery can be cured nowadays with modern drugs, and prevention depends upon cleanliness and good hygiene. I have sometimes had to treat monkeys that have been infected by the *Entamoeba* parasite.

Entamoeba, a disease-maker

How we get amoebic dysentery

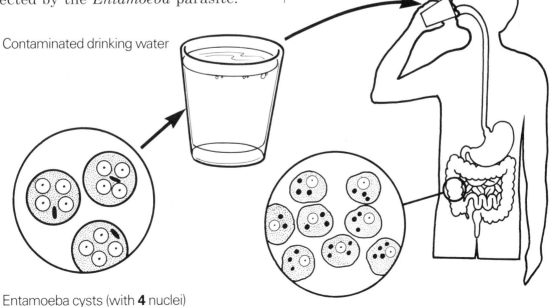

Contaminated drinking water

Entamoeba cysts (with **4** nuclei)

'Baby' entamoeba with single nuclei

The Medicinal Leech

An animal that is now very rare in Britain but that, given the chance, would love to be a member of the zoo in you is the *medicinal leech*. You are most unlikely ever to see one in the wild, and the chances of one attaching itself to you are even smaller, but the medicinal leech is included here as the sort of rarity that might be found in some more exotic zoos.

Leeches are members of the great family of segmented worms called *Annelida*, which are soft-bodied animals without backbones. They live on land or water and breathe either through the skin or by means of gills (like fish). The

than 4000 m above sea level. In the sea they are common parasites of fish, especially in the polar seas.

Leeches vary in length from about 5 mm to 45 cm, but their length and shape change frequently and dramatically, depending on whether their elastic muscular bodies are fully stretched out or not, and depending on

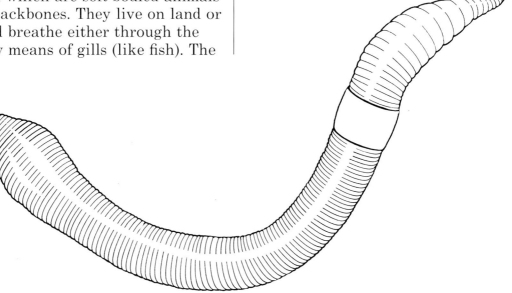

A typical annelid body-plan

body is divided into equal sections or segments and the skin of each segment sprouts bundles of horny bristles. The earthworm that lives in your garden is a typical Annelid.

Leeches are Annelids, but, unlike other members of the family, they do not have bristles. Their bodies always have 34 segments, they have suckers at both ends of the body, and they are all carnivorous or parasitic. They are 'hermaphrodites', having both female and male organs within the same body. Leeches live in fresh and salt water and on land, but all species need some water to survive, so they are not found in deserts, in the polar regions or higher

how much food they have inside them. They can appear like long ribbons, or can take the shape of an egg, a leaf or pear. Some exotic leeches are brilliantly coloured, with wonderful skin-patterns. They go on growing for 5 years and can live for up to 20 years. Although some leeches eat earthworms and insect larvae, most are full-time or part-time parasites who attach themselves to living animals and suck blood and body juices.

The commonest leech in Britain is the *horse leech*, which lives in ponds, rivers and canals. It is a dark ribbon-like animal that feeds on fish, amphibians and the bodies of dead animals. Other

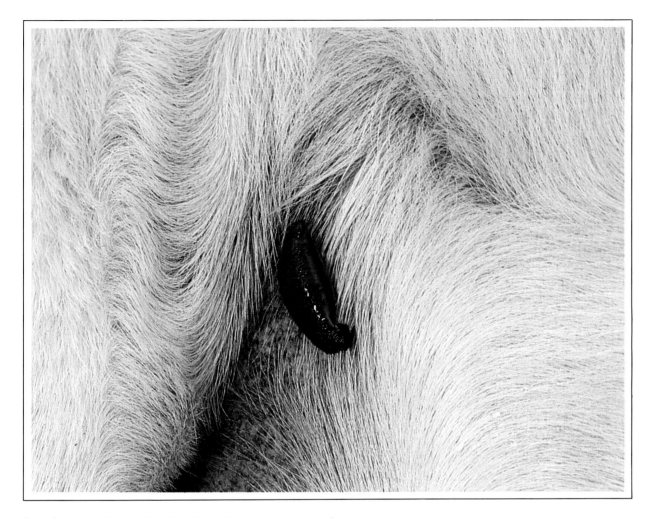

leeches seek out birds that live around water, such as penguins and ducks, or reptiles such as crocodiles and turtles. I have often seen the tiny scars of old leech-bites around the tail of the hippopotamus. There are species that live in springs and wells and enter the noses and mouths of drinking animals. They fasten themselves to the walls of the air passages and grow rapidly, making it difficult for the animal to breathe and causing bleeding. In India such leeches injure large numbers of buffalo, cattle, horses and dogs.

In the hot, damp jungles and rain forests of the East, *land leeches* occur in vast numbers, hanging from the twigs and leaves of bushes and trees and lurking in the undergrowth. They keep themselves moist by urinating upon themselves! Alert and active, they quickly attach themselves to their prey

A leech on a calf's skin

and will work their way in unnoticed through the smallest opening.

The medicinal leech is an animal with a long and remarkable history. This handsome dark-olive-green leech with orange markings was once common in Britain, but is now found there only in the Lake District in northern England and in the New Forest in the south.

Detecting its prey at a distance by means of its 10 eyes, its sensitivity to movements in the water and by its ability to detect tiny amounts of chemicals, such as those in sweat, it swims with wave-like wrigglings of its body and attaches itself to the skin of its victims by means of its suckers. The front sucker contains mouth-parts, including a set of 3 extremely sharp cutting-blades. Each of these is rather like half of a circular saw, and the 3 are set at angles of 60° to one another, making a perfect Y shape. The blades rock to and fro, and cut usually painlessly and always very quickly through the skin (though when I have placed medicinal leeches on my hand to watch them feeding I have always felt a slight pin-prick as they went about getting their lunch!). The leech releases into the Y-shaped wound a special saliva that contains a chemical that stops blood from clotting. This substance, called 'hirudin' after the Latin name of the medicinal leech, *Hirudo*, is of great medical importance

Digestion can take many weeks and isn't done by the leech itself. Instead it is done by a colony of friendly bacteria that the leech carries in its intestines and which do all the work of breaking up the liquid food. A leech can survive happily on just one such meal per year. Medicinal leeches prefer to take the blood of warm-blooded animals such as humans, cattle or sheep.

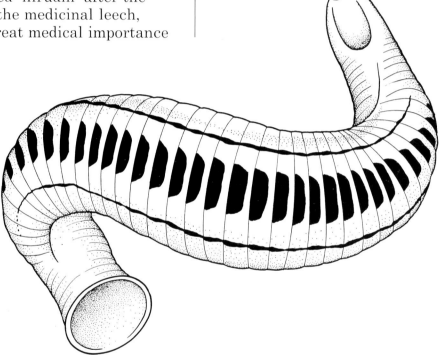

The medicinal leech

and has been studied and used by doctors for treatment of certain blood diseases in human beings. The leech saliva probably also contains some local anaesthetic, so that the victim feels no real pain. When the leech has made its cut it uses a muscular pump in its throat to draw out blood. Within a few minutes it is full and swollen up with about 6–7 cubic cm of blood and has changed from ribbon-shaped to roughly egg-shaped or pear-shaped. At this point it drops off its victim and sinks down in the water to digest its meal.

In olden days, when men and animals crossed rivers by walking through them or drank at ponds and riversides, it was easy for the medicinal leech to find its food. Changes in farming and the way people live have meant that cattle drink now at troughs in fields rather than from ponds, and men drive themselves and their livestock across rivers in trucks instead of on foot. Another important reason why there are now so few medicinal leeches is that in past centuries millions of them were caught for doctors to use in 'leeching' –

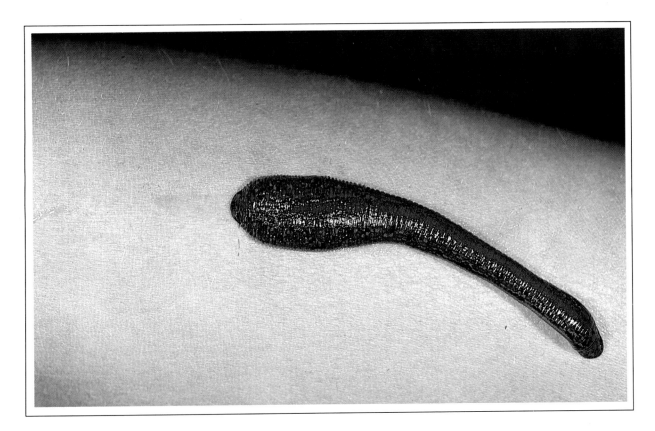

drawing blood off patients. This treatment was so common, right up to the middle of the nineteenth century, that doctors were themselves often called 'leeches'. Leeching was thought to be helpful in treating almost every illness, but we now know that in almost all cases it did no good at all. However, in a special situation where blood has to be drained from very delicate areas (for instance, around the eyes), surgeons will use the medicinal leech, whose delicate cutting mouth-parts are finer than any surgeon's knife.

People used to make a living out of catching medicinal leeches. Girls would wade into ponds with their legs bare and pick of leeches as they came and stuck to them, putting them into little wooden barrels that they carried slung to their waists. Doctors kept their stocks of leeches in beautiful china jars.

Leeches have a number of natural enemies, including birds and fish, particularly the perch and trout. If you are ever lucky enough to see a medicinal leech, don't be put off by its

A leech dining on my arm

vampire-like reputation. It is a fascinating and highly specialized sort of worm that has been used by man to play a major role in medicine over many centuries.

Leech girls collecting leeches

The Flea

A n occasional inhabitant of the zoo in you is an insect that according to the Book of Samuel in the Bible caused the Philistines a lot of trouble, and that helped to kill a quarter of the population of Europe in the Middle Ages! This is the flea, a true but wingless insect which lives on the skin of its host as a parasite. Fleas possess a tough horny 'shell' covered with many bristly hairs. They have mouth-parts that are specially designed for piercing and sucking, and hind legs that enable the insect to make incredible jumps. Because fleas feed on the blood of mammals (including man)

There are 1600 species of flea in the world. They can be found in the Arctic and Antarctic, in tropical jungles, in deserts and in towns and cities. Most are 1–5 mm long. The largest British species is the *mole flea*, which reaches a length of 5–6 mm, while the largest known flea is one that was found in a beaver's nest in the United States and measured 8 mm.

Some fleas will only live on one kind of mammal or bird – for example the *shrew flea*, which doesn't fancy

Body plan of the flea

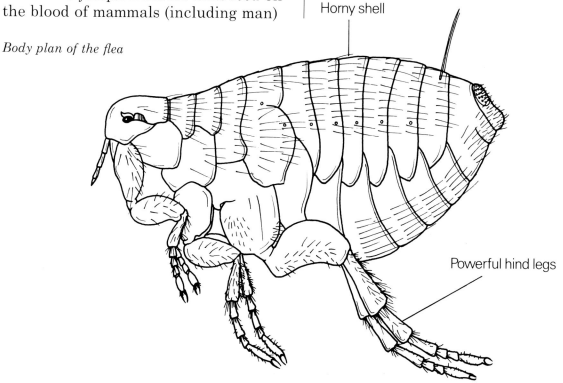

Horny shell

Powerful hind legs

and birds, they sometimes carry infectious diseases. This is how the *rat flea* spread the Black Death in the Middle Ages, causing 25 million human beings to lose their lives – more people than died in any other known epidemic or war. In the Far East and other parts of the world, fleas are still involved in outbreaks of plague among man and animals. They carry the virus that causes the terrible disease myxomatosis among rabbits, and also the tapeworm parasites that infest dogs and cats.

anything but shrews. Other fleas aren't so fussy; they prefer one kind of host but will sometimes feed on other species. *Cat fleas* prefer small cats, but will also visit humans, dogs, foxes and big cats, such as lions (Shakespeare wrote in *Henry V* about 'the valiant flea that dares eat his breakfast on the lips of a lion'). *Dog fleas* prefer dogs but can be found on humans or cats if dogs aren't available. The *human flea* prefers humans, but dogs and cats are also favourite hosts. The *chigoe* or *jigger*

flea, the smallest of all flea species, attacks humans, domestic animals and birds, and, while the male flea feeds on the surface of the skin, the female burrows beneath it and lives inside a little cyst or ball that grows around it. All fleas can cause itching and irritation of the skin as they feed, but the chigoe flea produces severe itching, burning and swelling, and is a serious pest in parts of tropical and sub-tropical America. Flea-bites on humans in northern Europe are generally quite harmless. They leave a small red dot surrounded by a light ring and are only slightly itchy. Apes and monkeys don't get fleas! Nor do horses and most hoofed animals. Rodents, on the other hand, have lots of fleas.

The human flea is 2–3 mm long and is red brown in colour and rather shiny. It lives for up to 2 years and can go a whole year without food, although it likes to feed every day if possible. Before mating, a female flea must have a meal of blood. Eggs are laid 4–8 at a time, with up to 400 laid over a period of

A cat flea on human skin

3 months on the body or in the bedding of the host. The eggs are white and oval but are not glued to hairs like those of lice. This means that they fall off the host's body very easily. The eggs hatch into tiny larvae in the form of grubs

Cat-flea eggs and droppings

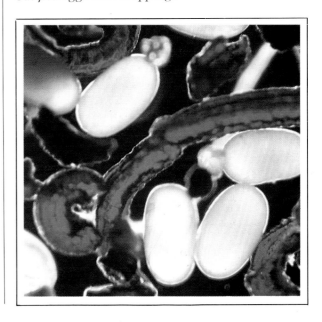

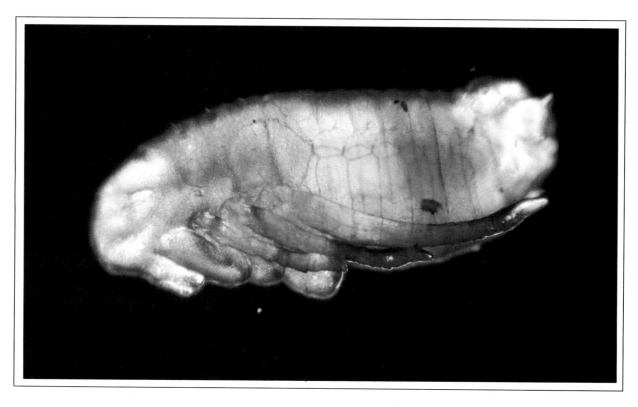

A cat-flea pupa

A champion jumper works out

which feed on dried blood, waste products, skin-scales and the droppings of adult fleas (which contain blood, of course). After 1–3 moults, the larva spins a cocoon and turns into a pupa.

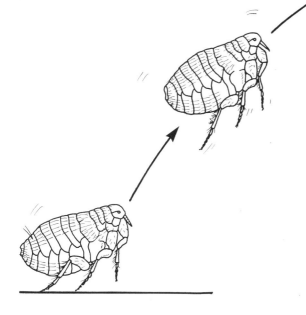

From the pupa a fully formed flea emerges 2 weeks to 8 months later, depending upon how warm it is. The complete life-cycle of the flea can range from as little as 14 days up to many months.

The flea has a body that is flattened on the sides; this and the backward-pointing bristles on its body help it to move through the jungle of hairs on the skin of its host. The human, dog and cat fleas have well-developed eyes. Bat and mole fleas have poor eyes, or no eyes at

Roll up! The flea circus!

all, and so prefer hosts that live in the dark.

The flea's hind legs enable it to jump 200 times its own body length. One flea athlete achieved a high jump of almost 200 mm and a long jump of 330 mm. To do as well as the flea, a fairly tall human athlete would have to jump a quarter of a mile! The power for the flea's amazing jump does not come simply from flexing muscles but from the sudden pulling-in of a special elastic-like chunk of tissue that stores energy when resting.

I was fascinated as a boy by the 'flea circus' that used to be seen at Belle Vue Zoo in Manchester during the summer. (I saw another one a few years ago in Munich). In a flea circus, human fleas (other flea species don't perform so well) walk tightropes of fine hairs, 'fence' with swords made of thin wire, pull tiny carriages and carry umbrellas a few millimetres long. The audience watches the show through large magnifying lenses.

The behaviour of fleas, like that of so many other wild animals, has been used in the past as a means of forecasting the weather. An old British saying goes,

When eager bites the thirsty flea,
Clouds and rain you sure shall see.

The Louse

And now to the lousy part of the zoo! Lice are fascinating creatures, but they can be a great nuisance too, and are certainly not the most pleasant animals to have in your personal zoo. Because of this, I am glad to say that these little pests are not as common as they used to be.

One day, the Scottish poet Robert Burns was in church and saw a louse crawling over the bonnet of a lady sitting just in front of him. When he got home he wrote a poem called 'To a Louse'. Here is part of it, and, to make it easier for you if you don't understand Scottish words, I shall repeat it afterwards in ordinary English.

Ye ugly common creepin', blastit wonner,
Detested, shunn'd by saunt an' sinner!
How daur ye set your fit upon her,
Sae fine a lady?

Gae somewhere else, and seek your dinner
On some poor body.

You ugly, common, creeping useless creature,
Detested, shunned by saint and sinner!
How dare you set your feet upon her,
So fine a lady?
Go somewhere else, and seek your dinner
On some poor person.

Lice are wingless insects with flattened bodies and are 0.3–11 mm long. They come in various colours, from white or yellow to brown or black.

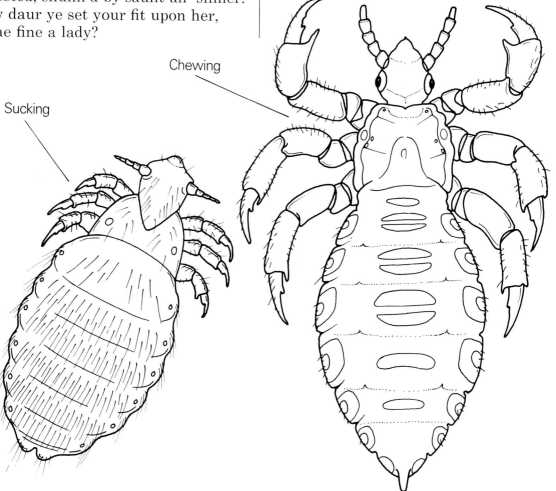

Sucking

Chewing

Sucking and chewing lice

There are two main types: *chewing lice*, which live on the bodies of mammals and birds and eat skin-scales, feathers, hair and grease, and *sucking lice*, which suck blood. There are almost 3000 species of chewing lice and about 400 species of sucking lice known to science.

Each species of chewing louse lives on a particular type of animal. For claw which they use to grasp the hairs of the host creature. The hold of the claws is amazingly powerful – a louse can resist a pull of 1 kg! Even if the body is cut from the head, the louse continues sucking for a while, and it can survive under water for a long time. (When a seal dives, *seal lice* take air down with them, trapping it between their scales and hairs.)

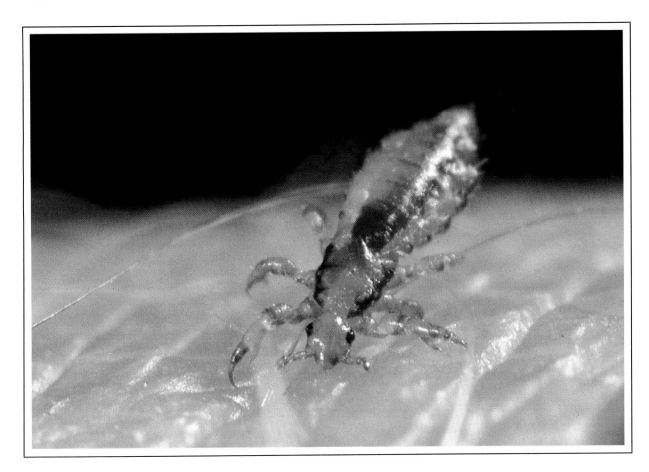

instance, *elephant lice* live on elephants and *lemur lice* live on lemurs. Some animals, such as bats, ant-eaters, armadillos and whales, don't have any lice.

Sucking lice are pests that are sometimes found on human beings and can carry diseases such as typhus in tropical countries. They feed only on warm blood and die within 12–72 hours if they don't get it (unlike fleas, which can go without a meal for as long as a year). Each of their feet has a single big

An adult head louse on my hand

As with chewing lice, specific kinds of sucking lice live on specific hosts. Some prefer rodents, others elephants, others man and the great apes. White birds have white body-lice, while black birds have black ones. Many animals and birds carry several species of louse at the same time, with each species living on one particular part of the body. Lice are attracted by the heat given out by a living animal and will walk towards a

body when they can sense its warmth. This they are able to do from a distance of up to 30 cm. Probably the smell of their particular host also attracts them. They also get about by travelling on clothing, on the wind or by hitching a ride on flying insects. As soon as they come into contact with an object, lice automatically try to climb up it.

Three kinds of louse live on humans: one likes to live in the pubic hair of the groin area (at the front, where your legs join); the second prefers the body hair, including that of the eyebrows and beard; and the third makes its home in the hair of the head. People used to think that lice came out of nowhere, created out of nothing. It was also commonly held that only strong, fit people produced lice – that they were a sure sign of good health! In the olden days lice were used in folk medicine, and as late as the last century people in the Lake District in the north of

A sucking louse at lunch

England believed that, if they swallowed a tablespoonful of live headlice, that would cure jaundice (a kidney disease in which the skin turns yellow). In the seventeenth century witches were sometimes accused of sending lice to people that hadn't suffered from them before, as a way of bewitching them. In 1645, a woman called Alice Warner who lived in Suffolk in the east of England confessed that she had sent evil spirits to carry lice to two women who had annoyed her. Sadly, the courts believed this nonsense and she was convicted.

The sucking louse has a needle-like sucking-tube (proboscis) in its mouth-parts. When not in use, it is pulled back into the head. When sucking, the proboscis is extended and drilled deep into the skin, while the louse literally stands on its head! Head lice have even adapted themselves to the different hair characteristics of various human races. The differences are in the shape of their claws. Some have claws that fit perfectly the hair-shafts of white people; others have evolved to grasp the slightly differently shaped hairs of black people; and yet others have evolved to live in the hair of yellow-skinned people.

the egg-cap to one side and jets them out of the egg!

These days, outbreaks of lice infestation occur from time to time in places where lots of people are in close contact. For example, such outbreaks sometimes occur in schools. The lice are a nuisance, but they can easily be got rid of by using special shampoos that kill the lice and the nits.

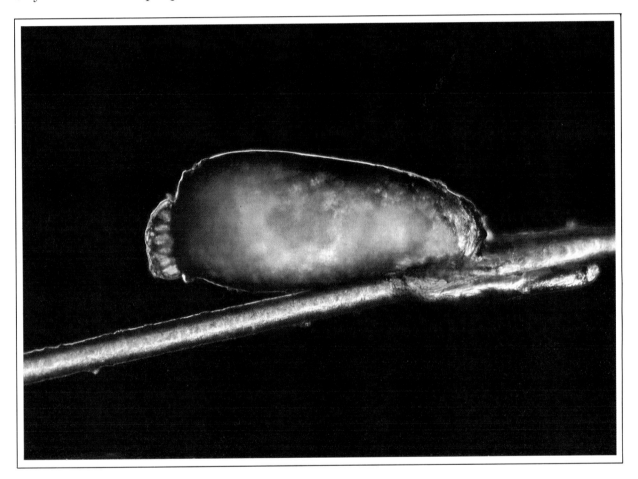

Lice lay eggs called 'nits' and glue them to the hairs of the host. Each egg has a lid in it which is fitted with air-holes. Up to 300 eggs are laid over a period of around 6 weeks. The larvae, tiny copies of adult lice, hatch after 1–2 weeks. They cut their way out of the egg using an egg tooth on the head. They then swallow air, as well as any liquid remaining in the egg, and in this way puff themselves up. Some of the mixture of fluid and air is then pushed out of their rear ends, and this pushes

A nit stuck to a human hair

Some primitive tribes people actually treat lice as sacred and precious. When the Spaniards conquered South America, Indians would often bring them purses full of their own body-lice.

Some animals live by preying on lice. In the Mediterranean area, some lizards survive on the lice to be found in colonies of seagulls, and others do the same among the cormorants that live along the coast of Peru.

The Roundworm

The world is overflowing with round little worms, and some of them are occasionally to be found in human beings. I'm not referring to earthworms, those familiar garden creatures that live in the soil and have

water, in soil, moss and decaying matter. Others are wholly or partially parasitic on plants and animals. One little worm, only 1 mm long, is called the 'vinegar eel'. It lives its whole life in beer-barrels, where it feeds on the yeast

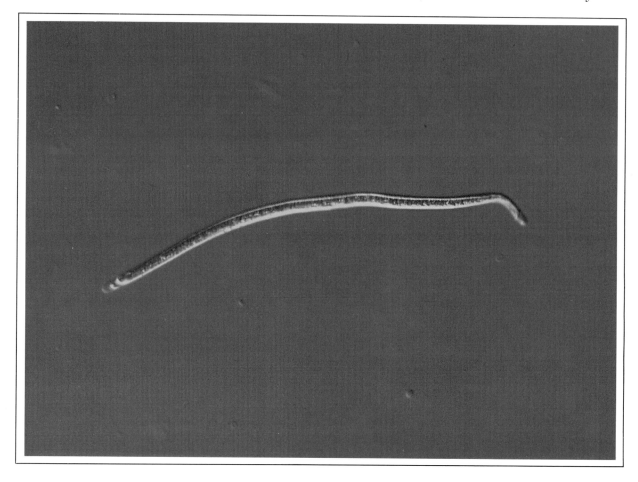

A typical roundworm or nematode

segmented bodies, but to another and even bigger group of worms, whose bodies are not divided into segments. These worms are whitish or translucent (light can pass through them) and usually tube-shaped. They vary in size from a fraction of a millimetre to over 8 m long! These giants live in the Pacific Ocean.

About 20,000 species of *nematode*, as scientists call this type of creature, have been identified. The earliest ones lived over 370 million years ago. Many, mainly the tiniest ones, are 'free-living' and do not rely on other things to provide them with food and lodgings, but can be found in both fresh and salt

used to make beer from hops and water.

It is amazing to think that the soil can contain as many as 100 million nematodes per square metre, and they are one of the largest groups of living creatures in the world. There are millions of them, and they can be found just about everywhere. It is said that, if all the buildings and other man-made structures on earth, along with all the trees and the rest of the plant life, were suddenly made to vanish, an outline of all of them would remain. For a moment, familiar things and places would still exist in a sort of ghostly form made up of the innumerable nematode worms that inhabit them. 'Houses' of worms, 'trees' of worms, 'fences' and 'bushes' and 'telegraph poles' of worms would all be visible, their shape outlined by these tiny yet wonderfully abundant worms.

The most troublesome roundworms are those that, as parasites of man and animals, can cause disease. Some free-living nematodes also attack the roots, stems and leaves of food plants and are considered a great pest by farmers. In hot countries hundreds of millions of people are infected by species of roundworm, mainly because not enough

you probably know that pet cats and dogs have to be 'wormed' from time to time – given a special powder to get rid of similar troublesome parasites that infect them.

Human beings in Europe and America are not often infected with roundworms, but several species do sometimes cause trouble. The *pin worm* is one of them, and its life-cycle is typical of that of many roundworm parasites.

Pin worms are parasites of human beings, apes and some other animals. They are sometimes found living in the bowel or large intestine of children, and usually do not cause illness or injury in

A pin worm's life-cycle

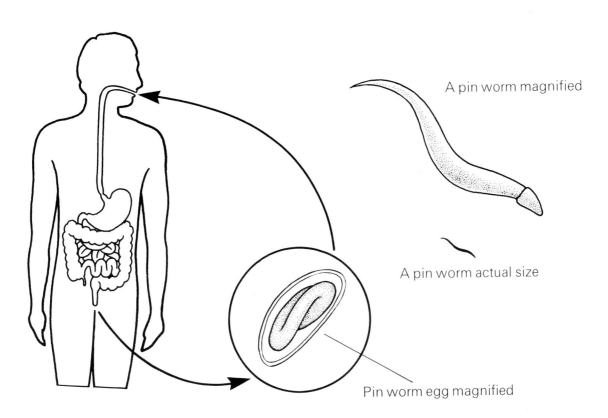

A pin worm magnified

A pin worm actual size

Pin worm egg magnified

care is taken to make sure that food and water supplies are free of these pests. In Europe and America, farmers have to keep a watchful eye on roundworms that can invade the bodies of cattle, sheep, pigs, chickens and turkeys, and

any way. Male pin worms are 2–5 mm long and are seen only rarely, while females are 8–13 mm long and whitish pink in colour. After being fertilized by the male, the female travels down the large intestine to the anus, through

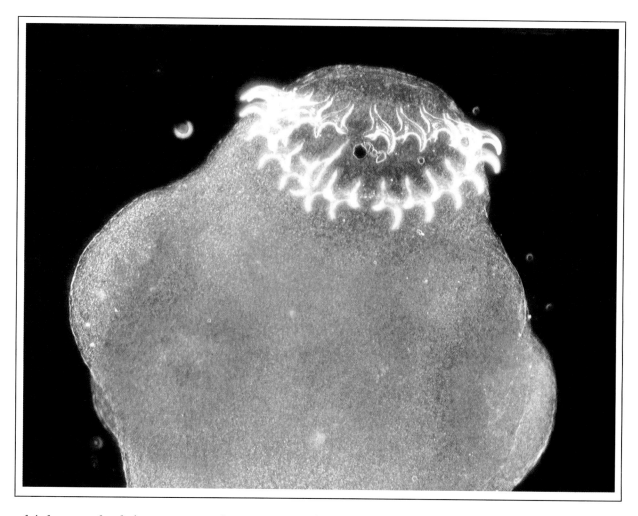

The head of a tapeworm

which your body's waste products pass out when you go to the toilet. When she gets there, she pops out and lays her eggs on the skin nearby. If you scratch this area and do not wash your hands, it is easy to carry the eggs or the larvae that hatch from them to the mouth, where they are swallowed and pass down into the large intestine. The full life-cycle takes between 2 and 6 weeks to complete. This worm spreads with great ease from one member of a family to another, and doesn't only infect people who don't keep themselves clean and tidy. Fortunately, modern medicines kill the worm rapidly and soon put an end to any infection.

Some roundworms such as the pin worm just feed on food around them in the bowel. Others actually suck blood from the wall of the bowel, and there are some dangerous species whose life-cycles include wandering journeys by the larvae through the deep body tissue of the liver, where important damage can be caused.

Two other major classes of worm can sometimes infect human beings. The first, the *tapeworm*, is a parasite whose body is flat and ribbon-like and composed of a tiny head attached to a chain of compartments that look a bit like the segments of segmented worms such as earthworms but are actually separate units joined together. Each segment or 'proglottid' contains masses of eggs. The life-cycle of the tapeworm is not as simple as that of the pin worm. To develop properly, the larvae must find temporary hosts such as pigs or fish. Man is infected by eating pork that has not been cooked long enough or by eating raw fish. (Raw fish is a food often eaten in a number of countries, including the Scandinavian countries and Japan.)

The second class of worms, rare in humans, is the *fluke worm* – a leaf-shaped parasite that, like the tapeworm, has a complicated life-style and needs temporary hosts for its larvae. Snails are often hosts of fluke-worm larvae. The fluke worm is a serious parasite of sheep, in which it mainly attacks the liver. I often see another kind of fluke worm living fairly harmlessly in the stomach of dolphins.

Roundworms are quite long-lived. Many species reach 15 years of age, and there are reports that some nematodes that live as parasites on plants can live for as long as 39 years.

In the seventeenth century, the Dutchman Anton van Leeuwenhoek was the first man to use a microscope to study some of the tiny living creatures in his own body and in the world around him.

After examining vinegar-eel nematodes he wrote,

'I have had several gentlewomen in my house, who were keen on seeing the little eels in vinegar; but some of them were so disgusted at the spectacle that they vowed they'd never use vinegar again. But what if one should tell such people in future that there are more animals living in the scum on the teeth in a man's mouth, than there are men in a whole kingdom?'

A typical fluke worm

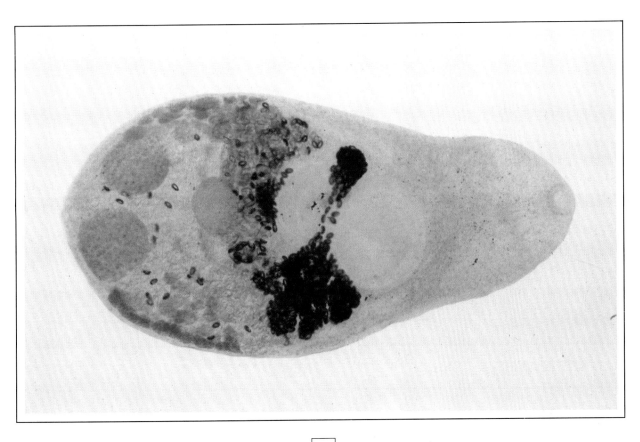

The Mite

In your skin, particularly that of the eyelids, some distant relatives of the scorpion are living at this very moment. These are the mites, members of the family of animals called *Arachnida*, which includes scorpions and spiders. Unlike insects, they have 8 legs, not 6. Some mites live in the sea, others on land. They can be found from the Arctic to the Antarctic. Some, such as the ones that belong to the zoo in little damage, wandering about through the dried upper layers of the skin. Other species burrow deep into the skin and cause serious swelling and burning. Some prefer to live in animals' outer ears, and are a common pest among pet cats and dogs. Mites that affect some kinds of birds can even penetrate deep into the body, reaching the lungs and

The mite's body-plan

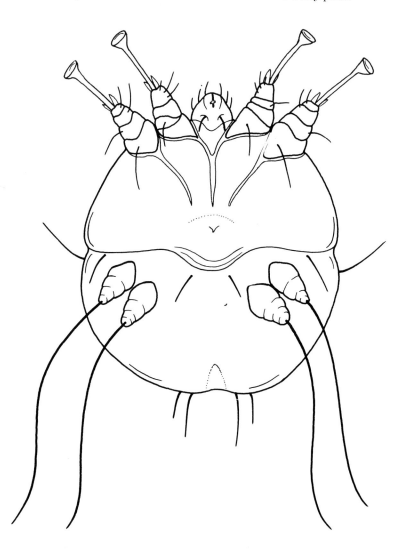

you, are parasites, and are the smallest of all arthropods (creatures with joints in their legs) known to science.

Mites that burrow into the skin of mammals and birds cause a disease called 'mange' ('scabies' in humans) by feeding on scurf and skin-scales and sucking blood. Some mites cause only a air-sacs, though in fact they don't cause much trouble when they get there. Some mites lodge in the body-surface of man and other animals without attracting any attention.

One of these is called *Demodex*. It is your constant companion, always to be found in your personal zoo. Only about

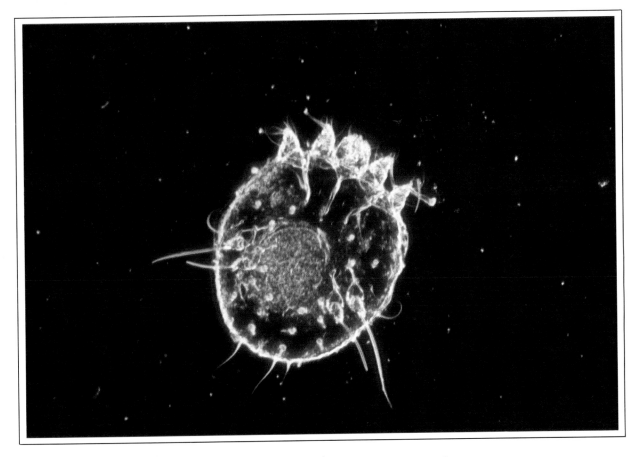

Sarcoptes, a mite that causes mange

0.3 mm long and shaped like a cigar, it has short, sucker-like legs and is usually found lying head-down in hair follicles (the little pockets from which hair grow), squeezed between the hair and the follicle wall. In this position it scarcely moves, but it can, if it wants, march at a speed of around 375 mm per hour. It is particularly fond of the eyelids and the follicles from which the eyelashes spring. As many as 25 mites have been found down one human eyelash follicle! A normal 'population' of mites in your eyelids is about 1–2 for every 16 lashes.

Mites of both sexes are to be found in the hair follicles. Mating occurs close to the entrance to the follicle. About 10–15 hours later, the female descends and lays her eggs in the grease-secreting gland under the follicle. The eggs are only about 0.075 mm long and are heart-shaped. After 2–3 days they hatch and the larvae emerge from them looking something like the adult mite but

Demodex loves eyelids

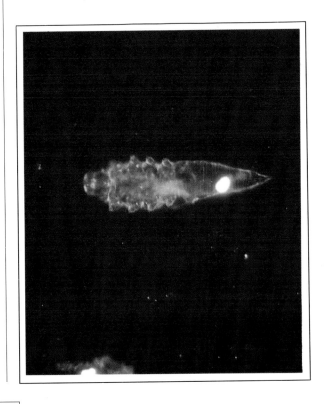

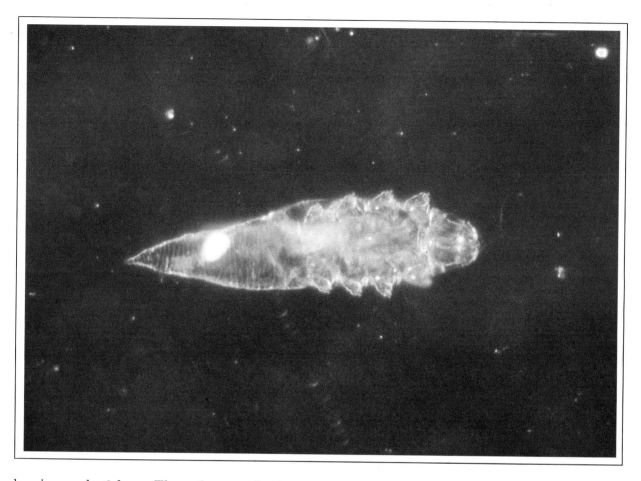

The eyelash mite, Demodex

having only 6 legs. These larvae shed their outer casing after around 2 days to produce an 8-legged 'protonymph', which in turn moults its shell after a further 3 days to become a 'deutonymph'. This creature has weak legs and cannot keep a firm hold of the hair, so it gets washed to the surface of the skin with the grease from the gland under the follicle. The poor little thing is then obliged to wander about on the surface of the skin for a day or so before finding a follicle into which it squeezes and in which it moults again to become an adult mite. The total lifespan of a mite is about 2 weeks.

Sarcoptes is the name of a mite that often causes mange in animals and occasionally produces a similar complaint called scabies in humans. At about 0.4 mm long, it is slightly bigger than Demodex, and also has a different shape: under the microscope it looks rather like a tiny tortoise. Sarcoptes digs into skin using the front two pairs of legs, which have cutting blades fixed to their 'knees'. The backward-facing spines on the body also help it to burrow, which it does at around 3 mm per day. As the female tunnels, she lays 2–3 eggs every day. These eggs are oval and white, and as many as 30 of them can often be found dotted behind the female along her burrow. This digging in the skin causes itching and burning, and scratching can introduce germs into the skin and set up bacterial infections. Mange and scabies are successfully treated by doctors and vets nowadays. Sheep are dipped in special solutions to prevent mange, and humans and other creatures can be treated by special shampoos, creams, sprays and even tablets.

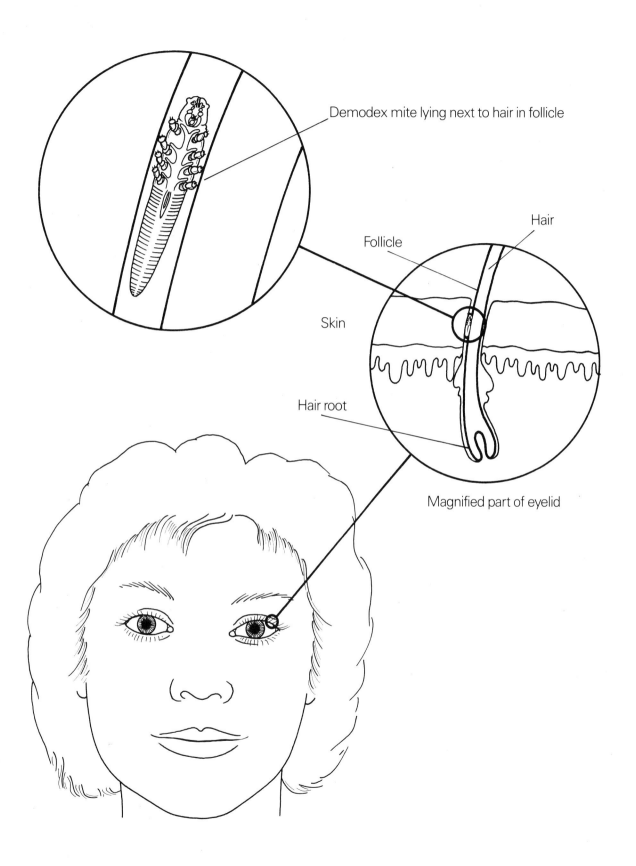

Demodex mite lying next to hair in follicle

Hair

Follicle

Skin

Hair root

Magnified part of eyelid

The mite that lives in eyelids

The Malaria Parasite

We have already looked at the amoeba, a form of protozoan animal that lives commonly in the intestines of human beings and is usually harmless. Another kind of protozoan can live in humans, finding a home with the red cells of the blood. It causes a disease that is no longer native to Europe, and does not normally occur outside the tropics, but which has been responsible directly or indirectly for *half* of all human deaths since the Stone Age. This protozoan, a mere dot when viewed under a high-power microscope, is the malaria parasite, which still kills at least 1 million people each year in Africa and Asia. Other animal species, such as apes, monkeys, birds (particularly penguins) and reptiles, can suffer from kinds of malaria.

Malaria in man is transmitted by mosquitoes of a particular group called *Anopheles*. 3 species of Anopheles mosquito, capable of carrying malaria,

live in Britain, but can only carry the disease if they happen to come into contact with someone who already has it. No natural cases of malaria have occurred in Britain since the 1940s. Before that, soldiers returning from fighting abroad in the First World War (1914–18) had brought back the disease with them, and malaria-carrying mosquitoes made their home in marshes not far from London. Now, when people in Britain are diagnosed by doctors as having malaria, they are people who have recently been travelling overseas to places where mosquitoes still carry the disease.

In days gone by, malaria, a disease in which the patient suffers from high fever and sweats a great deal, was common in Europe. It used to be known as 'ague'. The earliest records of the disease date back to the fifth century

A malaria-carrying mosquito

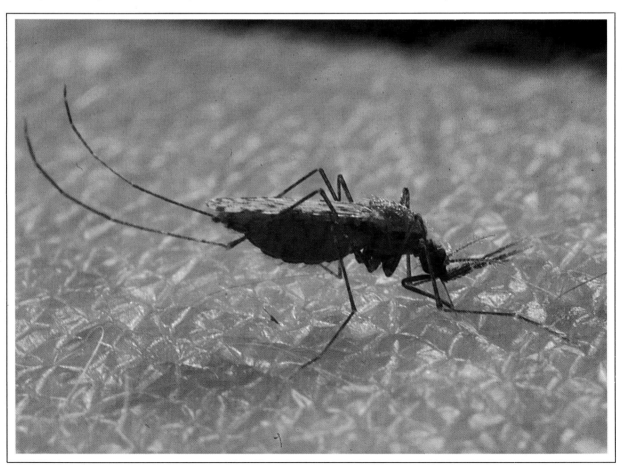

BC, when the Greek physician Hippocrates wrote about various kinds of fever. Some historians believe that widespread epidemics of malaria helped to cause the fall of the Roman Empire! The word 'malaria' comes from the Italian for 'bad air' and it was long ago

creatures in the water. So that it can grow, the larva sheds its outer casing 4 times, and after that it hardens into a pupa. After 3–4 days the pupa hatches into an adult mosquito. To begin with the mosquito drifts around using the pupa case as a raft while it waits for its

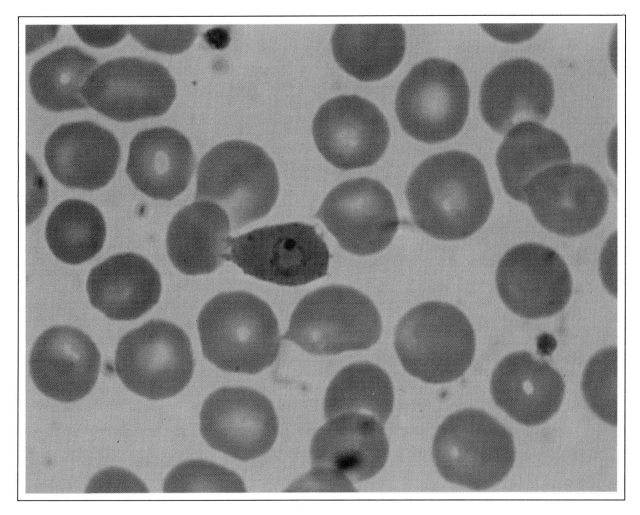

Malaria parasites in human blood

thought to be caused by just that. It isn't, though the damp air of marshes and other bodies of water provides mosquitoes with the water they need in order to breed. Both the malaria parasite and the mosquito need man to be able to survive and prosper.

Mosquito eggs are deposited in water. After 2–3 days the larvae hatch out, and they spend the next few weeks near the surface of the water, breathing air through a sort of snorkel tube (like that used by deep-sea divers) at both ends of their bodies and eating tiny living

wings to dry. When it has dried out properly, it is able to fly. Once in the air, male and female mosquitoes mate, and then, while the males go off to feed on plant-juices, the females set out in search of human blood! The female mosquito has piercing and cutting mouth-parts and injects saliva as she feeds on her victim. If the victim is suffering from malaria, the malaria parasite is present in the blood and enters the stomach of the mosquito as

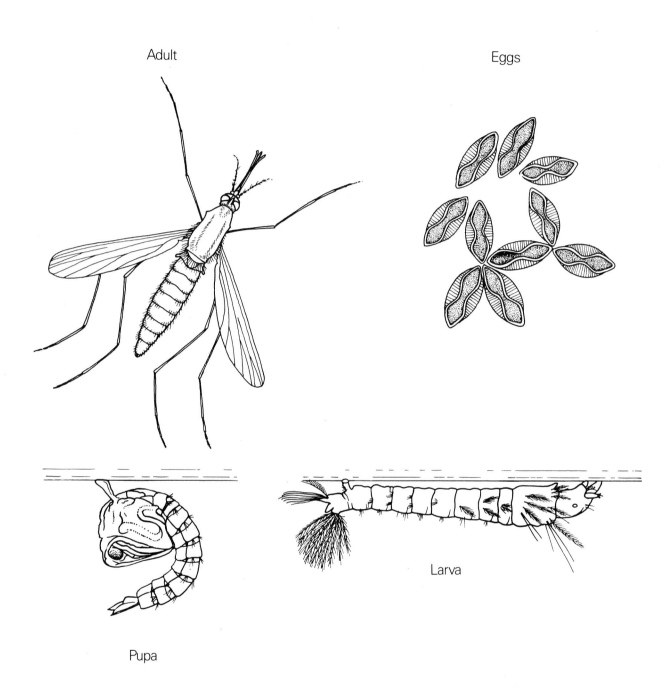

Adult

Eggs

Pupa

Larva

she feeds. Once it is there, the tiny protozoan undergoes changes and multiplies over a period of 1–3 weeks. The malaria parasites then move to the saliva glands of the mosquito. When the female mosquito takes her next meal, the parasites are injected into the victim with her saliva. They travel through the blood to the liver, where they multiply again and then invade the red blood-cells, where they multiply yet again. The multiplying of the parasite breaks open and destroys the red cell. It is the damage done to the liver and the red blood-cells that causes some of the main symptoms of malarial disease.

Quinine, a medicine produced from the bark of the cinchona tree of South America, began to be used to treat malaria around the beginning of the eighteenth century, long before the cause of the disease was known. It proved very good at controlling the disease. Now other drugs are available, but some parasites have been able to used to kill the insects, and, by sleeping in beds covered with netting, people can be protected from mosquitoes while they sleep. Again, people visiting areas where malaria is still common can take tablets to protect themselves before leaving home. A recent idea is to treat male mosquitoes with atomic radiation so that they cannot fertilize the females and the females' eggs cannot produce new mosquitoes. This could hardly be

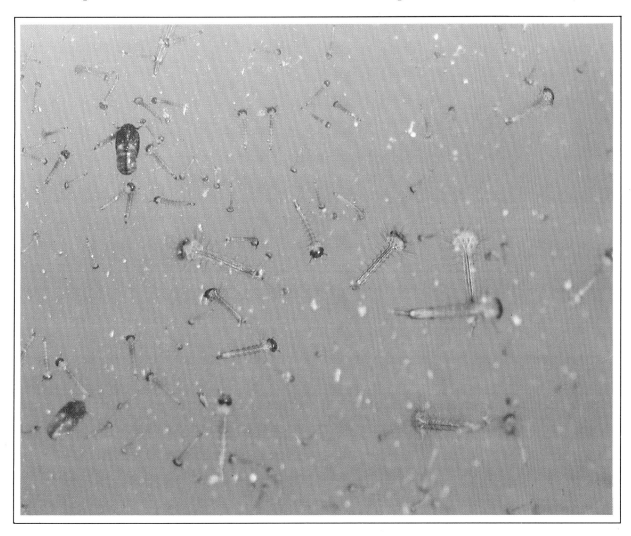

Mosquito larvae in a pond

develop a resistance to them.

Prevention of malaria depends most of all on controlling the mosquito population. A number of measures have been found helpful. These include draining stagnant pools of water, treating water reservoirs by adding special chemicals, and encouraging fish that eat mosquito larvae. Sprays can be

done with all male mosquitoes, but it might prove helpful as the females only mate once.

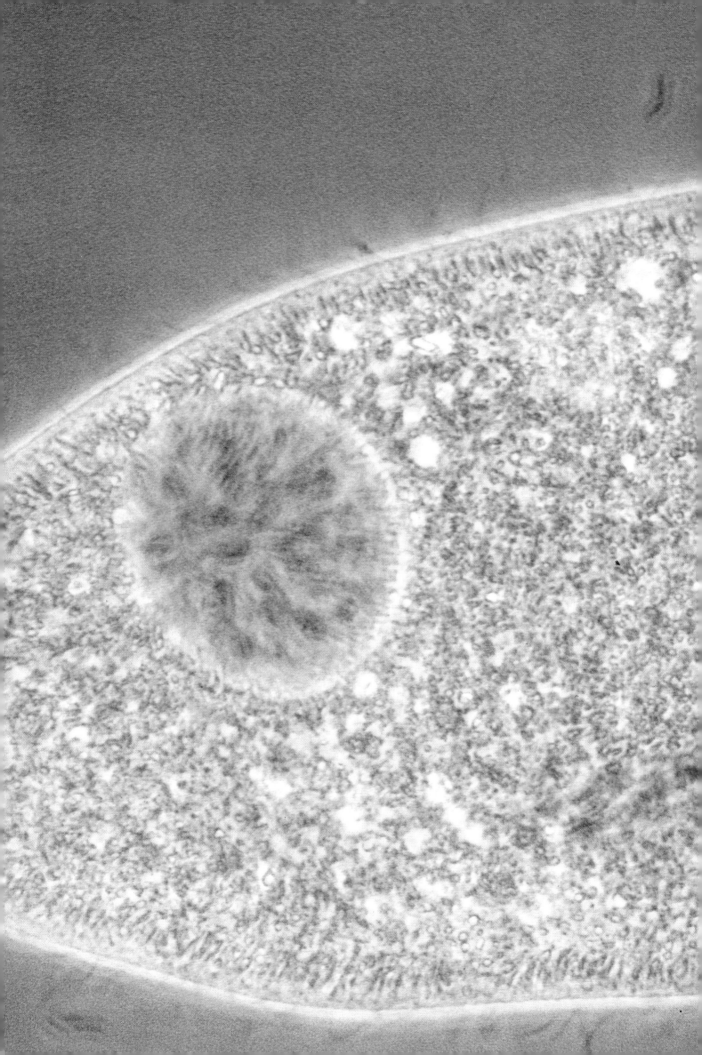

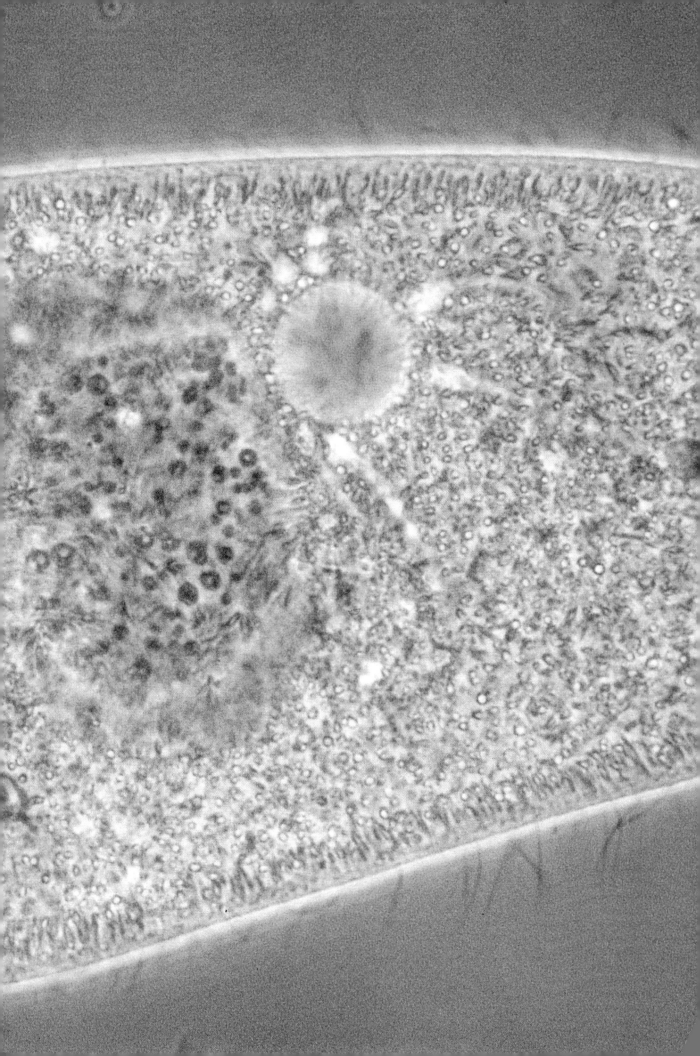